HERE IN MY SENSES

Edited by

Andrew Head

First published in Great Britain in 1998 by
POETRY NOW
1-2 Wainman Road, Woodston,
Peterborough, PE2 7BU
Telephone (01733) 230746
Fax (01733) 230751

All Rights Reserved

Copyright Contributors 1998

HB ISBN 1 86188 616 0
SB ISBN 1 86188 611 X

FOREWORD

Although we are a nation of poetry writers we are accused of not reading poetry and not buying poetry books: after many years of listening to the incessant gripes of poetry publishers, I can only assume that the books they publish, in general, are books that most people do not want to read.

Poetry should not be obscure, introverted, and as cryptic as a crossword puzzle: it is the poet's duty to reach out and embrace the world.

The world owes the poet nothing and we should not be expected to dig and delve into a rambling discourse searching for some inner meaning.

The reason we write poetry (and almost all of us do) is because we want to communicate: an ideal; an idea; or a specific feeling. Poetry is as essential in communication, as a letter; a radio; a telephone, and the main criteria for selecting the poems in this anthology is very simple: they communicate.

Many of us had a special place when we were a child, the bottom of the garden, in a local park, even a favourite friend's house.

The poets in this book have written about their special places, telling us how overwhelmed they feel when they think of this place and try to help us capture the essence of this too.

This collection of excellent, meaningful work is a pleasant, easy reading book which leaves us all thinking of past happy memories of special times to each of us, whatever they may be.

CONTENTS

Scotland	G M Cookson	1
Midsummer Meeting	N Mary McCaig	2
Country Lane	Rose Skelson	3
Spar Lake	William Ailbe O'Neill	4
Our Gift Of Smell	Thalia Kent	5
A Personal Oxford	John W Dossett-Davies	6
Land Of Life	Olive Irwin	8
Past And Present	Olive Bedford	9
A Visit To Bath	Jean Hendrie	10
First Night At Batu Gajah	J C Fearnley	11
Keele Bluebell Woods	Peter James O'Rourke	12
My Pleasure	Heather Agius	13
A Walk In The Deserted Bay	Carol Ann Hill	14
Hyacinths	Rita Robinson	15
Orkney	Lena Hilton	16
The Long-Lost Dance	Joan Hands	17
Mighty River	Jennifer H Fox	18
A Nature Garden	N M Beddoes	19
Midnight On The Common	Pauline Hepple	20
The Forest Path	Hazel Wilson	21
Vista Coll De Rates	J D Bailey	22
Spirit Of The Past	Nicholas Armstrong	23
Enchanted Peace	Diane Simpson	24
The Silver Birch	Lisa Wolfe	25
Home Farm - Summer Of '96	Pauline Fogerty	26
I Won't Recall	K Bocking	27
Another Place	Timm Dorsett	28
Life In Prison	J K	29
Rachel's Room	Mary Care	30
Tranquillity	Cathy Bulley	31
I Remember Still	Pamela Girdlestone	32
A Stream	Sheila Margaret Dell	33
Untitled	J C Harwood	34
Solitary Contentment	Elaine Hawkins	35
A Candle's Glow	Margaret Winrow	36
A Kitchen In Town	Jules Ward	37

I Love You	Thelma Kellgren	38
Child Hide!	Florence Andrews	39
Ferris Wheel	Alan Simmons	40
A Place Called Heaven	Debbie Avery	41
Iona	D S Chalk	42
Reminiscence	Alison M Rowan	43
I Shall Tread These Welsh Valleys . . .	Amanda-Jane Martin	44
Saturday Evening, Aberdeen Beach	David Tallach	46
Childhood - Memories	Ingrid Bockmann	47
A Conservatory Contemplation In November	Ada M Witheridge	48
Evening On The Avon - Despite The Bypass	Rachael Clyne	49
River Skell	Robert D Shooter	50
Vesperella	Gail Vernon	51
Not In England (Time Travel)	Ruth Bettany	52
Woodland	Lyn Richard	53
French Restaurant	Elizabeth Parish	54
Raining Again/ Wondering Weather	Alis Rain	55
Behind	Rebecca Lawrence	56
Quaint Streets	Gordon Carter	57
Eastbourne . . .	Anne Clark	58
The House	Guy Fletcher	59
For Jackey's Pen	Paul Davis	60
The Loft	Joe Hughes	61
Side Street	David Medcalf	62
To The High Places	S H Smith	63
Radcliffe Weir	R L Cooper	64
Sunsets	Valerie Marshall	66
My England Isle	M Millard Bradley	67
Preston Docks	Jim Patten	68
Shall This Be The Last Time That I See Ireland	Margaret Gleeson Spanos	69
A Quiet Storm	Graham Macnab	70
Sketches Of Skipton	John Carley	71

A Holiday Paradise	Anne G Wallace	72
The Garden Swing	M D Reader	73
Hollywell's Arboretum	N D Potter	74
The Place We'd Meet	John Hill	75
A Sense Of Cheshire	Pat Derbyshire	76
At Seven	Kate Sumner	77
From Lower To Higher	Claire-Lyse Sylvester	78
Change	Ivy Cawood	79
Delhi India	Doreen Welby	80
Dreaming In Acharseid Mor	Bill Waugh	81
The Grand Canyon	Jessica Jordan	82
Song For A Seagull	Lee Sheldrake	83
The Village Church	Joan Mackereth	84
At Budds Wall Bedhampton	Jennifer M Trodd	85
In My Glory	Robert Wilkie	86
Torre Abbey Sands	Janette Coombe	87
Dawn	A R Bailey	88
Survival Of The Skylark	Keith Dickinson	89
Britain's Glory	Bessie	90
This Blessed Land, This England	Thomas Victor Healey	91
Rhossilli	David J Hall	92
Flattenden Wadhurst	Edith Buckeridge	93
Memories Are Mine	Brian R Russ	94
At Dunn's River Falls, Jamaica	Ian Bramley	96
The Magic Wood	Joyce Morris	98
Such A Place!	Tricia Rozze	99
Pray For Me	Sue Williams	100
My Beach	Eric McClurry	101
Stormy Seas	Maureen Annette Norman	102
Island Of Dreams	Winifred Mary Richardson	103
Northern Australia	J V Galvin	104
The Waves	Emma Ormond	105
A Country Stroll Recalled	C J Norton	106
Out Of Africa	Elizabeth Hunter	107
Feather Flowers	Richard Holt	108
To Rest Beside	Ron Grantham	109
Brighton Beach Memories	Susan Utting	110
Poppies	Winifred Thorpe	111

Colours Of The Mind	Zita Holbourne	112
From Snowdon's Summit	Roger Williams	114
Your Sky This Evening	Joan Marian Jones	115
The Meadowland	Ross Alexander Omand	116
The Yellow Flag (Iris)	Mike Cohen	118

SCOTLAND

Your majestic hills make the spirit soar
Like the eagles wing over many a moor.
Dusky gold in the evening's sun
Freedom for the soul to run.

River torrents gouge their course
Rushing through with mighty force.
Mountain reaches into cloud
Snow-capped like a mantle proud.

Each glen dips in homage given
To the pinnacles reaching heaven.
A loch lies silent as the grave
Or sparkles in the sun's bright rays.

A river's crag with dark foreboding
A sunlit glen the heart to roam in.
Bog and clay on Culloden's field
Stir the soul in sorrow yields.

Towering peak above Glen Coe
Monuments to battle long ago.
The vale of tears still holds sway
Renewed with fervour each new day.

A kirk stand silent its watch to keep
Protecting all its scattered sheep.
Wind whips through both heart and mind.
Carries you back through space and time
O' Scotland you will always be
A land to dream in eternally.

G M Cookson

MIDSUMMER MEETING

I met the Giant of Cerne Abbas today
His silence spoke - in peculiar way -
'Tell them about me, and who I am -
Tell them about their own ancient man
Who guards their Wessex land!'

I gazed up at this Giant . . .
He's not brooding . . . just gentle!
He strides west over hillside, with purposeful tread
Genial yet watchful, with unerringly accurate
Lines drawn with power from his feet to his head.

I felt safe, with this Giant, old man of the people
Figure eternal, who guards this fair land,
Known to tribes of Durnavaria under Roman legions
Know to royalists, to martyrs, to men of all seasons
Like Nelson's Hardy, RN - Thomas Hardy, famed writer
Known by centuries of Greenwood Romany bands -
Known by peasants and smugglers,
By painters and dancers
And by all of old Dorset's folk - romancers
Like Will Barnes, poet rustic, whose verses made music
Of the dialect of his time!

In sweet silence I heard him -
For I did not fear him
This protective earth-spirit still holding strong sway,
Bringing all into focus, through past into future
I'm so glad that I met that good 'Giant' today.

N Mary McCaig

COUNTRY LANE

To stroll along a country lane
On a late summer afternoon
With family and friends
    Is happiness
The laughter of children as they run before you
Adds to the joy in our hearts.

The once golden fields of wheat
Spread out around us
The harvest is gathered
The ploughs long-since gone
Only fields of burnt stubble remain
Until another summer.

We notice not the grey hazy sky above
But each little flower that grazes by the wayside
The pollen of plants
As they float on the wind
Like balls of gossamer silk
In the soft warm air
Across fields and hedgerows
To bloom again
        Another summer.

Rose Skelson

SPAR LAKE

Diamond droplet on the Shield, sacred spawn of Mother Earth;
Tree-encrusted jewel where nature fair abounds.
Restful haven heaven-sent to stoke the genesis of mirth,
In weary hearts defiled by city grind and strident sounds.
To cavort in clear water and pull fishes from below;
To see an osprey cruise above and hear the plaintive cry of loon;
Whirr of hummingbirds recedes and bullfrog calls now steady grow;
Shooting stars streak the sky and distant wolves howl to the moon.
Pleasant banter on the shore, we eager watch marshmallows roast;
But it's the water, the warm water, I remember most,
I swear before my God, some day a jaunt again I'll make;
To sup friendship with the Cochranes at their cottage on Spar Lake.

William Ailbe O'Neill

OUR GIFT OF SMELL

If we stop to remember our bygone days, to recall the days of old
Our sense of smell will serve us well as memories unfold.
What person can fail to remember the smell of new-cut hay?
Of playing in the meadows on a warm and sunny day?
The smell as we came in the door. Mother's made a cake,
Scrumptious pies and crusty bread, what care she'd always take
I remember as a child living by the sea.
The smell of rotting seaweed still serves to remind me
Of happy times in childhood. I also loved the coffee shop
Where coffee beans were grinding, I always used to stop
To smell the beans roasting. I feel as tho' I'm there
My memories come flooding back - the aroma fills the air
Outside that shop . . . but time has marched on by
And now that I am older, I often wonder why
When people see the wonder and beauty of a rose
They fail to give the credit to the one who created those
Wonderful flowers, honeysuckle, azaleas, which fill us with delight
'Twas God who gave us our senses, touch, smell, taste and sight
So let's not take these things for granted, let's give Him His due praise.
And thank Him that we have these gifts,
                    which make meaningful our days.

Thalia Kent

A Personal Oxford

It is suffused with memories
I a student
Went to hospital
Met the dark-haired nurse - Jeanette

All one summer
We walked, talked and boated
And went to the cinema
And took tea at Fullers and the Cadena

She was twelve years older than I - and divorced
She knew about the ballet, books and life

After six months
We had a trivial tiff - and drifted apart
In due course
I left Oxford
And for years never thought of her again

Fate has brought me back to Oxford
I walk the familiar streets
And begin to see her again
Glimpsed in the distance in Christchurch meadow
A face partly seen gazing from a Headington bus
The back of a head at the Playhouse
A figure crossing Magdalen Street
As I stare incredulously from Debenham's teashop
Where we used to go when it was Ellistons

There she is still, dark-haired, tiny with big staring eyes
Quite unchanged
Only, of course, it's not her -
Just girls who look like her
With young men who look like I did
All those long summers ago

What should I do?
Lay the ghost that stalks me still in Oxford
By visiting her
And risk disillusionment
Or enjoy the apparition that has become my personal Oxford
Now I have returned?

John W Dossett-Davies

LAND OF LIFE

The green grass of home,
The sandy deserts of Saudi Arabia,
The deep jungle forest of South America,
The tropical island of Tahiti,
The wild and dangerous lands of Africa,
The romantic city of Paris,
Each one has a destiny of life
Dreams, enchantments, treasures
and wild spirits for wild lands of love.

Olive Irwin

PAST AND PRESENT

Take my hand and I'll escort you from the present to the past,
At Salmesbury Hall your memories will for ever last
This mighty Tudor mansion enhanced by shady boughs,
The finest layout for antiques each room delights to house.

At the desk in the entrance hall you pay a small fee,
Behind which a large fireplace with priest's hole you can't see.

The oak floor it shines with no hint of neglect,
Decades of good living its strength does reflect

There's a room where a lady inspired from above,
Gave life to some children she carved with great love.

The priest's room is steeped in reverence and awe,
Where strong men brought low betwixt peace and their war.

Come quickly down the wide staircase my lines have almost gone,
No time to look in other rooms for pieces you wish to bid on.

We've reached a room the heart of which is a table huge and oblong,
With open fire and chandelier and feeling you belong.

A focal point in present days is this table's centrepiece,
Fresh, simple flowers from herbaceous beds arranged with
                                             natural expertise.

There's also a cafe that fulfils mortal needs,
High chairs and good food, scones with cream teas.

I know this Hall is thankful and proud of its success,
Reborn to serve millennium heirs sharing mutual respect.

Olive Bedford

A Visit To Bath

The Baths, were built by Romans,
With sandstone from the town,
And altho' you can view the remains today,
Most of the buildings have crumbled down.

The source of the water, is a natural spring,
Which was meant, to cure, all ills,
And the Royals, were brought, to bathe in it,
Instead of taking, pills.

'The Abbey', the Royal Crescent, and the museums,
To mention, just a few,
Are some of the historical places,
Thousands of visitors, come to view.

You can take a boat trip, on the river,
And browse in shops, both large, and small,
Also take the time, to have a walk,
Around 'The Grand Assembly Hall'.

The Royal Crescent, designed, by John Wood,
Where famous people, would stay,
Still has a house, at 'Number One',
And visitors view, its contents every day.

There are lots, of steep streets, in Bath,
Which are really hard, to climb,
But during my three weeks' holiday there,
I had an enjoyable time.

Jean Hendrie

FIRST NIGHT AT BATU GAJAH

The heavy cloying fragrance
Of unseen exotic blooms
Pervades the tepid air,
While the silence of the jungle
Composed of a thousand sounds
Filters through the barbed-wire coils
Which crawl in stark relief
Across a giant setting moon.

Moon-set, and such darkness!
As palpable as velvet on the cheek.
Or is it just the thick warm breeze
Creating the illusion? Within the tents
From every quarter of the camp
The snorts and snores of sleeping men
Repel the creeping silence.
A comforting cacophony, eagerly embraced.

At last with eyes accustomed
To even such black velvet depths
Heart-shrinking terror as the bushes sway,
A refuge for assassins; or is this too the breeze?
The watch seems endless, every nervous hour
Oppresses more the soul, which craves the light.
So the first faint flush upon the eastern rim
Elates the spirits, and the nascent orb
Is greeted as perhaps in ancient times
When the old ones seemed never to be sure
If they would ever see its rise again.
That night, I will confess, I had my doubts.

J C Fearnley

KEELE BLUEBELL WOODS

When springtime comes to this great land
And pleasure fills the mind,
A bluebell scene and straightaway
I'm back at Keele I find.

A springtime carpet blue bedecked
To captivate the eye,
A royal show, a woodland hill
A village nestles by.

Keele Bluebell Woods in springtime bring
Life to our village scene,
And proudly with her bright blue robe
Is England's Woodland Queen.

With squirrels, hedgehogs and foxes
On magic bluebell ground,
Where nature gives them all a home
Away from fearful hound.

Rejoicing splendour fills the woods
With songs the song birds sing,
Sweet melodies in bluebell time,
Keele choir on the wing.

Return I must in heart and mind
To beauty I commend,
When bluebell magic senses touch
And greets me as a *friend.*

Peter James O'Rourke

MY PLEASURE

The garden of childhood is a wonderful place,
Full of sunshine and laughter, beauty and grace
Favourite flowers, all shades and hues,
Bright golden daffodils, forget-me-not blues.
Snowdrops and crocus, endless delight
Fruit trees in blossom, red pink and white.
Butterflies dancing, adding beauty and pleasure
Busy bees humming, as they gather their treasure.
The pollen so yellow, the nectar so sweet
Help to make honey, oh! What a treat!
Lying in the sweet grass, not a care in the world,
Smelling the scents of flowers, watching nature unfurled.
To capture this moment and keep it forever
The memories of childhood, would be very clever
But we can if we slow down and listen and look
Go into the garden, find a nice nook
Sit down, relax, look around you and see
The garden, recapture, the child that was me.

Heather Agius

A WALK IN THE DESERTED BAY

The bay is tranquil and deserted today,
All the intrusive visitors have gone away,
The tide is out, and a gentle breeze blows,
And dog and I, are out for a morning walk,
The sparkling blue sea is murmuring nearby,
With gentle waves breaking over golden sands,
While seagulls shriek and circle overhead,
And the tang of sea salt on the breeze,
And just for once time stands still,
Then the wind from the sea begins to moan,
And sends up rough tossing waves,
With foaming white sea spray,
And my imagination runs wild,
With tales of pirates, smugglers and mermaids,
Which fascinate and intrigue people everywhere,
And abound in every village and cove,
Along this rugged Celtic Cornish coast,
But time encroaches on my quiet peace,
The uneasy sea begins to storm and rage,
And pounding waves batter craggy rocks,
And dog and I must take our leave,
Before the fury of the sea storm breaks,
With one last look at the surging seas,
We hurriedly leave the deserted bay.

Carol Ann Hill

HYACINTHS

A heavy scent pervades the air
And suddenly I am not there
The beautiful colours and strong perfume
Have taken me back to my first classroom
The wooden desks with a tip-up seat
A little bar to rest your feet
The blackboard, the duster and the chalk
You went to school to learn - not talk!
The walls were painted two shades of green
With a dividing line between
And all around the lofty wall
There was a shelf above us all
Open fire with a fireguard
You 'went up in class' if you worked hard
Children didn't arrive in cars
And we used to recycle old jam jars
But the thing I most remember
Is that each year - around November
Every child within the class
Would grow a hyacinth over glass
The bulbs would all be hidden away
Then we'd arrive at school one day
And on that shelf all round the wall
And sometimes even in the hall
The hyacinths had appeared on view
In shades of pink and white and blue
Each morning as we went through the door
The scent was stronger than before
So still each year - when hyacinths bloom
I 'spend some time' in my first classroom.

Rita Robinson

ORKNEY

Come visit Orkney, there's so much to see
Arrive on the ferry or choose the plane
Or even the short route, the Pentland Firth
All the verges filled with wild flowers,
No one to tread them down, born free to stay free
Primroses, violets, orchids and such

You can see blood-orange sunsets
Sweetness and mellowness of late summer days
The sounds that come, we hear people call
'We're here the Northern Lights'
Winters are magic in Orkney, millions and millions of stars
The ever-changing moon

Harvest time in Orkney, come meet our people, join in the fun
I'm sure it won't take long, to know everyone
The winter sun hangs over the ridge of Coolag, this seals
our shortest day

Winter the sun now pale between shades of darkness
We now gather our peats, to sit round the fire
Hot soup, tatties, sharing our tales
Soon it will be spring again, the gorgeous days to capture
Out with the brushes, to paint the scenes, come rain, wind or snow

Like a carpet the celandine, wrens dashing by
A lonely daisy, pushing its way up from the peaty bank
The spring has now appeared, bulbs showing colour
Blues, mauve, yellow, what an embracing sight

May is like a beautiful romance, mist, sun, wind and rain
Reaching out, bringing our beautiful Primula Scotia
Come now, Orkney is part of your wonderful world

The birds make their call, the seals sing to you
At dawn you will hear them, it's time to take note
All you have wanted, peace and tranquillity, that's *Orkney* for you.

Lena Hilton

THE LONG-LOST DANCE

Hark to the sound of gypsy music
the swinging hips and the tapping toes
swirling crimson skirts,
man and woman
the inevitable bond
of healing within the inner self.

I see myself in some far-off land
swaying to the timeless music of my soul
as in a dream
guiding me to that nectar of human love
immortal, incalculable, but free.

Time unbidden lends a hand
to recall
the sensuous meanings
of that lovely gypsy music
still in my soul.

A long-lost loved one,
but never lost
swirling crimson skirts
flounced and gay
twirling my heart away.

Joan Hands

MIGHTY RIVER

I go down to the Rhine from time to time
I love this old river, its barges and brine.

From a Swiss mountain source it wends its way
the falls of Schaffhausen through a sunlit ray.
Glimpse, the grey rock of Lorelei maiden fair
who lured boatmen to death with her golden hair,
through the ages the Rhine stirred the fancies of men
past castles and vineyards, three score and ten.

Follow its path as it turns with the tide
coals and chemicals hitching a ride.
Viewed from above it curls like a braid
past churches and chimneys plying its trade
through industrial city and flooded plain
rippling in sunlight, drab grey in the rain.

Take a turn on the tow-path walking and lazing
see shepherd and sheep drifting and grazing,
a riverboat trip with afternoon tea
pretend you are drifting down to the sea.
On the last stretch as it runs its full course
through flatland and flower field gathering force.

The power of the Rhine as it ploughs its way
remember it well, for some distant day.

Jennifer H Fox

A Nature Garden

Through Shropshire's sylvan glades I strolled
Along a shaded lane,
And in a clearing I beheld
A garden, which in main
Was covered with a vernal growth
Of springtime fortitude,
And as I gazed my heart extolled
At nature's aptitude.

The close cropped lawn, soft to my feet
Like carpet fresh from loom,
Was bordered by a tiny patch
Of dainty plants in bloom.
The timid crept towards the grass -
A vain protective wall;
The bolder stood as sentinels
On guard behind them all.

I gently touched a budding flower
And was trapped in a spellbound trance
By the song of a bird, and the tune of a bee,
And a kiss from the breeze of chance.
For it was chance that held my hand
Along the woodland way
To nature's pretty garden plot
Where I return in dreams today.

N M Beddoes

MIDNIGHT ON THE COMMON

The flaxen moon, so round, so bright,
Illuminates the starry night;
The clouds go scudding 'cross the sky,
Like silken veils, they float so high,
Dark, serried ranks of poplar trees
Sigh and whisper in the breeze;
And way out in the distance - hark!
I hear a hungry fox's bark.
An owl's bright eyes search out his prey -
He'll eat his fill 'ere break of day.
Walk onwards, over dew-moist grass,
Leaving crushed footprints as I pass,
And wander down towards the pool,
Deep and tranquil, ever cool;
The creatures startle in its depths,
As gravel crunches 'neath my steps.
The calm, the peace within this place
Renews me for next day's rat-race.

Pauline Hepple

THE FOREST PATH

The path winds its way through the forest.
Weary of lingering shadows, trees raise their foliage
to the sunlight rays.
Rain stays covering the forest floor in crystal water beads.
Lush green grasses gleam as rain gently bathes each blade.
Ferns in multitude, waving and bending as a breeze struggles
to absorb the rivulets.
In the dark shade, pearls of dew rest undisturbed, insects come to
life murmuring and crawling midst twigs and bracken.
Quietness and coolness send a sense of peace
in the forest's heart.

Hazel Wilson

VISTA COLL DE RATES

The high piny woods scent the air;
A bird of prey leaves its lair.
A tiny village in the valley beneath
Reflects white light like rows of teeth.
The distant sea, coloured an azure blue,
Blends into skies of a diff'rent hue.
A winding road climbs up forever:
What better view could I discover?

J D Bailey

SPIRIT OF THE PAST

As raw twilight forsakes the lonely dell,
And wishes day a stern farewell.
Song birds crying, swoop into leafy jade.
No soul stirs, but spirits wade.

Strident gusts malign the lifeless leaves,
Which droop downward devoid of need.
And the moon, night's only torch,
Shines resplendence on a forsaken chapel porch.

Amongst the ancient headstones,
Death chants its unsung shroud,
By which we, mere mortals,
Are inevitably bound.

And despite the earth is lacking day,
A spirit walks which lights the way.
Only there for some to see,
But maybe, it is only me.

Nicholas Armstrong

ENCHANTED PEACE

The water trickled down the stream
In the misty forest clearing
Into the pond where fish swam freely
As the birds chirped quite cheery.

An anxious doe and her fawn
Came to the clearing just after dawn
They sampled the luscious dewy grass
And nibbled berries from the bushes they passed.

The rustling trees brought the cool wind
Throughout the misty forest clearing
It startled the deer and they ran quickly
To find the stag for protection and safety.

The stillness of the forest mist
Engulfed the clearing to the ridge
Where the mountains reach up high
To the sun, rising gently, in the sky.

Diane Simpson

THE SILVER BIRCH

It stands in my garden, a massive sight
With its thick trunk a creamy white
Its crown reaches an enormous height
The branches spread out, a canopy wide.

The miracle is how it took root
In the centre of a terrace where a birdbath stood
A little bird must have dropped its food
And so planted the seed that grew into wood.

One day we noticed a stem had grown
Sticking right out between the stone.
We waited impatiently till it had shown
What kind of a plant our garden had won.

The next year we found to our surprise
That it was a birch tree about to arise.
Had we known it would grow to that size
We might have thought leaving it unwise.

It went on to grow, its crown to unfold
In spring its catkins are a sight to behold
The leaves in autumn turn into pure gold
We are so glad we let it grow old.

Lisa Wolfe

HOME FARM - SUMMER OF '96

I sit here in silence alone on the fell,
the past weeks of summer what a story to tell
there's the planning and shopping and loading of car
for our weekend retreat that's so near yet so far.
Then I remember a story a friend of mine wrote
about the brackens and Romanies, the little Egypt they sought.
Is this then our Egypt this farm we all love
all the fun and the laughter as I watch from above.
The children run barefoot their faces aglow
down to the river, where they swim and they row
the sound of their chatter vibrates through the trees
as they splash and they play in the warm summer breeze
Then it's time for the wood hunts
there's a fire to be lit
the bigger the fire
the longer we sit.
The children are sleepy they gaze at the stars
there's talk of spaceships and landing on Mars
Soon one by one they trot off to bed
they stifle their yawns and goodnights are said
then we all gather round, the drinks they are flowing
some have a coffee to keep themselves going
the wood dwindles away and the fire starts to wane
so we burn all the rubbish, only a few of us remain
there's a stillness around us, just a flicker of the fire
we're reluctant to leave but sleep we require
The animals are stirring as the sun starts to rise
so we trundle to bed with red weary eyes
so this is my story, of our Egypt, our heaven
Let's hope there's a sequel (Summer '97).

Pauline Fogerty

I Won't Recall

Deep valleys, paths made of stone
Finest memories of times spent alone
Cross-roads, endless mazes
Childhood and all its phases.

Your subconscious, the playing field of the mind
We carry on playing even though we are confined
I won't recall the times I've had sadness
When I've bent over backwards and dealt with my madness.

When thoughts are crippled with times of the past
When I thought in my mind that those memories were cast.
I won't recall even when I fall, I'll never remember
I'll try not to feel, let my feelings be denied and
                                      believe they're not real.

Times you tell yourself, it'll all work out fine
The past is forgotten, the past is not mine.

K Bocking

ANOTHER PLACE

I sit alone on the verandah,
Overlooking the pond,
The rushing of the water as it cascades,
Playing a soothing song,
And as the sun descends from the sky on its lazy journey,
It's goodnight goodbye,
The scent of the flowers reaches my nose,
Making my eyelids feel heavy,
Why, heaven only knows!
And as the gentle breeze rustles the reeds,
The night-time animals all come out to feed,
Leaving the birds to sing their final chorus from
                                        the trees beyond,
As I sit alone on the verandah overlooking the pond.

Timm Dorsett

LIFE IN PRISON
(Dedicated to JC Rose and Robert)

Being held inside is the hardest time to do
Because it's in prison it's hard without you
I keep myself so busy trying not to cry
But when I said it was easy I am telling lies

Every day is one done, of my time without light
I mark the day off, on my calendar each night
It doesn't get easier, though people say it will
If only I was coming back down that steep hill

My room is a hiding, for which I have the time
It's not the same as home, because it's not mine
My life is mapped out from daybreak, till dawn
When it's hot, one pleasure, is lying on the lawn

Even that is conditioned, as to when and where
Some days I feel that, people just don't care
I miss you so much, it hurts in my head
The only comfort exists, being asleep in my bed

Will you be there, when I am myself?
Or will I be left, on that empty shelf?
Don't let me down and don't let me go
Or my feelings, will drop to an ultimate low

I love you so much, and I want you to see
So when I come home I want you to be
There waiting to help me along
As you and I will have to stay strong!

J K

RACHEL'S ROOM

Her bedroom is a special place
where I can peep into her world,
with reverence I tread carefully
to keep her dreams intact and curled.

A girl who likes to be alone,
her contentment papers the walls,
she paints the colour of her soul
on canvas fields and waterfalls.

The tinkle of the mobile bells
swaying and sparkling in the breeze
brings echoes of her girlish laugh
and filters through the air with ease.

Empty wine bottle candle-waxed
stands on the bookcase dull with dust
Shakespeare's next to Little Women,
in childhood days she grew to trust.

Pinned to a board in disarray
a clutch of treasured memories;
old tickets from football matches
and favourite pop group Oasis.

CDs line the wall by her bed,
make-up and paintbrushes in pots,
Peacock feathers and scarves and drapes
gently soften my tangled knots.

With a smile she bids me welcome
whenever I happen to stay,
although she's not at home that much
I can feel she's not far away.

Mary Care

TRANQUILLITY
(Loch Lomond)

Beauty like a whisper
A silver shimmered sigh
Soothing, soft translucence
Stirred as a wind breathes by

Tranquillity of morning
Peace from deep inside
Serenity of being
With you I need not hide.

Cathy Bulley

I REMEMBER STILL

On a warm and hazy day,
When I was feeling lazy,
A knock at the door
'Twas my friend for sure
Fulfilling his promise to me.

On that sun-spilt morning
'Come' he said 'time's right,'
Bewilderment crept over me
For what my eyes were about to see
Was a truly wondrous sight.

I left my house, and turned the key
So as to lock the door
Down the path I followed him
His old face with its toothless grin,
To his house we went for sure.

He took me to the cellar
Down the stairs that moved and moaned
To a rusty door, that was old and worn
Would I ever see a new day dawn
In this silent world not known?

In old George's cellar
Specks of mould grow overall
The lights are dim
But the sun creeps in
Through cracks here and there in the wall.

Black sacks vast and shiny,
A secret is held within,
With musty air warm
It won't take me long
To gather these mushrooms with him!

Pamela Girdlestone

A STREAM

The stream below a Cottage-thatched,
Glides gently on its way;
Beneath a bridge of wood flowed she,
Upon a summer's day!

Rippling o'er the pebbles,
With sand upon her banks;
Flowers dip to her on either side,
Thirst-quenched - they proffer thanks!

Brilliantly, the water flows
Her everlasting way;
Past valley, hill and woodland;
On to Sandy Bay!

Cascading silver waters,
Beneath a moonlit sky;
Where hunting Owl swoops down for prey
Emitting shrillest cry!

So on she glides, from East to West
Desiring movement - scorning rest;
Contented, winds the Silver stream,
Through the country of my dream.

Sheila Margaret Dell

UNTITLED

I wander on this lonely beach
feel sand ripples with my feet;
sparkling pools
edged with green
and slimy rocks
covered by the water's flow;

Rushing tide
edged with froth
and submerged wood,
seagulls waiting
for scraps of food,
or flying through
the sparkling air;
hazy blue
fade to gold
Shade your eyes
against the sun;

Murmur of surf
rising heat
gentle lapping at your feet,
prickle of sand
coarse sharp rock;
seek the shade
in the warmth
Under the trees
revel in the favourite
haunt
of solitude.

J C Harwood

SOLITARY CONTENTMENT

Warm sun beating, hope the pleasant glow will last,
Sweet-smelling honeysuckle, a purple fuschia blast,
In solitary contentment, on a snapdragon sits a bee,
Path covered in dying blossoms,
that have fallen from a once overflowing tree.
Distant rumbles in a virtually cloudless sky,
Smoke trails from a plane that passes up high,
Winds blow gently, softly sway the trees,
One of summer's last butterflies floats past me,
Flowers in full bloom, soon to wither and die,
Soon no more burst of colour to please the tired eye.
Sun on my skin, I smell sweet scented blooms,
Heady is the mix of summer's strong perfumes,
People, traffic, sounds rudely invade the air,
I let them pass without thought or care,
As long as the autumn, it stays away,
Contentment I hold on summer's last day.

Elaine Hawkins

A Candle's Glow

Deep in the heart of a family home
The flickering flame of a candle glows
A means of light on a dark stormy night
Casting long dark shadows on ceilings and walls
Its warming glow casting its quivering light
Offering gentle comfort as the evening falls
As the wind down the chimney howls and blows
And windows and doors creak and moan
With rain bouncing high off pavements and roads
And lightning flashing with fierce bite
Putting terror into the frightened hordes
Until silence prevails again in the darkness of night
What value then in a candle's glow
As warmth from the flame touches body and soul
Caresses the hearts of all who behold
The soft shimmering light of a candle's glow.

Margaret Winrow

A Kitchen In Town

Splendid circles swirled inwardly
The cookie jar was vast.
Breadcrumbed orange peel fell
Softly down upon the upturned umbrella.

Wet newspaper makes merged words
The doormat has retired now.
Ornaments strewn, minestrone soup
And a block of white unsliced
Stands firm, refusing to be moved
off its spot.

The radio crackled into life
The afternoon wore on.

Jules Ward

I Love You

How could I have left you?
How often I have wanted
to come back.
It was all so long ago
But the yearning never died.

The sound of the screen door
Slamming,
The black-eyed Susans,
The hollyhocks
Those beautiful white birches.

Your sky so high, so clear
The air, the lake, the hayfields.
I now know
I will never forget,
New England - I love you so.

Thelma Kellgren

CHILD HIDE!
(Dedicated to sailors at sea)

You know that fearful feeling in the air -
Child! You must run! Run! Run!
Find somewhere to hide from here,
From us today I fear some dear ones shall be gone!

Run! Run! Hear it now on the air!
Tempestuous, savage wind gone wild,
Do not ask why, find shelter child!
The games wind plays are fearful, not fair.

Hide until this wild thing is done,
Wait for the quiet gentle breeze to come,
Now you must shelter awhile from the storm,
In time will come comfort from Mr Sun.

This world holds for children such terror and fear,
In the midst of their sweet innocence and laughter,
Desperate mother love tries to tell them beware,
Ever saying, 'I love you darling, take care.'

Florence Andrews

FERRIS WHEEL

You can see forever if you wish
Inside this defiant world that raises you
With your barest emotions, releasing
Unconvincingly.
The earth appears tenuous, adumbral;
To be alive is here, where we fall in love
At the topmost peak.
And what is love come full circle?

Alan Simmons

A Place Called Heaven

When darkness comes just as a thief
To encumber me with all my grief
I find some relief within your home
For in heart I am as one and free to roam.

And when I rise up from this place
I see a love shine in your face
Though you are nowhere near in sight
I feel your presence within my light.

'Tis you alone who's heard my cries
Every time my spirit dies
'Tis you alone who heals my pain
That I may rise and live again.

Debbie Avery

IONA

Salt-coloured sand,
common, intricate shells,
jagged, striated rocks,
variegated, polished pebbles,
spray spouting, rainbow-hued,
heather, resilient, restful;
firm tussocks, solid rock,
among the life-giving water.

Tarmac roads, single track;
bridle-paths or farm tracks, sparkling;
sheep tracks through the machair;
cow tracks through the bogs;
firm sand, washed clean by the tide,
dimpling under our feet;
pebbles, crunching, turning, sliding,
we change their patterning unnoticeably.

D S Chalk

REMINISCENCE

When the white cloud sits on the mountain top
And the earth grows hard and dry;
When the grass is brown with a withering
Then my thoughts will wander, fly
To a greener place where the bluebells grow,
Where the roses smell of rose;
Where the scents are keen and the senses too,
And there's tingling in my toes;
Then my feet will tap and my eyes light up
In recalling youthful days
When we danced with joy on the gentle sands
In the summer's soft sweet haze.

But the white cloud waits on the mountain top
And we are old and withered too,
So the dreams we have are the joys we share
In a love bestowed on few.

Alison M Rowan

I Shall Tread These Welsh Valleys ...

I shall tread these Welsh valleys that are my home
And walk their presence, as they clasp my winged flight.
All the burdens in which ate this once earthly heart,
Are now left to perish like the sheets of a cold night.

Do not grieve this tomb now that I have gone
Shed no more rainy tears, only the relief of smiles.
For I have finally returned at his waiting side,
Alas! Two lone souls reunited into one endless song.

I shall wander in exclaim upon the voiceless heath
And send you a comforting light to sweep your doom.
The eyeless trees which fondly bend their heads,
Will suffocate your darkly shades of mourning gloom.

Clouds as clear as the seas, unfold a cluster of memories
That roam green fields adorned in an enriched earth.
Her sights, her sounds do shake the sleepy rocky hills,
And my spirit is blessed with their Welsh air mingled in mirth.

Saints clothed in arms like dripping blood upon a flame
I hear footsteps climbing the cliffs hauntingly.
Ah! Such loyalty given, now at rest within those hilly brows,
I see the dragon had fired! Gripping my thirsting immortality.

My contented heart shall beat among the heroic veiny soil
Their flesh long-since devoured within dusted cries.
I will feel the pulse of every rising wave sent by the flame,
When sat in chambers of watchful, guarded eyes.

Place my listless wreaths and scatter them in the breeze
For their scent shall whisper kindly by my beloved's side.
And my spiritual harmonies will undress your sleeping yearning,
For it is among these valleys my heart must abide!
And my arms shall embrace the beauty in which Wales
                                        has bore
Their raging winds shall raise the standard high!
Thus sowing her seeds of ceaseless reign forevermore.

Amanda-Jane Martin

SATURDAY EVENING, ABERDEEN BEACH

Lighthouse winks on the headland
Promising a haven for weary vessels.
A boat with a beacon sails on the tide,
Away out for the herring, in the salt and smack of spray.

From long ago men fished in the local waters,
At war and peace with nature
Depending on the weather and the omens;
And the sacrifices of a summer solstice.

Oil-rig looms on the horizon,
Piping to the heartbeat of the seabed.
It must be lonely to live on a storm-tossed
Artificial island, an industrial maze of girders.

The coming of the Norse-men was foretold
From a lone visionary hut on the hill
By an old man, his hermit hair rough and ragged:
The rocks and pools were black with the foretelling.

I shelter by the barnacled wooden barriers
From the chilly spits of drizzling rain.
The beach is covered in a constellation of pebbles,
Surrounded by seaweed nebulae.

Olaf the Terrible and his vulpine crew landed
Amidst other long-ships, with their smell of death.
Battle raging on the cliff, a black funeral pall of smoke
As the new tenants occupy the smallholdings.

Briny sea pounds ceaselessly on shore land,
Life-belt keeps a lookout for those in distress.
The wet slip-sand darkens beneath my feet
As I turn and walk away from the incoming tide.

David Tallach

CHILDHOOD - MEMORIES

The flat is grey and dim, the furniture poor,
but the people inside, they are quite sure,
that their life is happy and very content,
even if it is hard to find the rent.
There is loving and laughter and happiness too,
have you ever found other more nicer things to do.
The flat is half empty,
no carpet on the floor,
but every 5 minutes there's a knock on the door.
Friends coming and going,
they are all having fun.
There is not much food,
but they do what they can.
Who says you need material things to survive,
if you've got family and friends
you will have a good life.
The little girl looks round,
a smile on her face -
have you ever seen a happier place.

Ingrid Bockmann

A Conservatory Contemplation In November

The day had dawned two hours ago but still
At eight o'clock a dull, dreary and greyish sky
Was looming overhead - a portent of the day to come?
A lowering, misty haze obscured the distant hills
And the drizzling rain gave windows and doors
An apparently permanent, bespeckled appearance -
Thus defacing the normally unblemished vista.
A magpie approached a distant fir tree
Soon to be followed by its mate -
Both seeking shelter from the elements.
Nearer, a magnolia, still in leaf, provided a haven
For a variety of other birds seeking sanctuary.
Looking ahead one can observe the effects of a
Brisk breeze - bending and buffeting the taller trees;
Whilst nearer the freshly pruned apple
Waved its now leafless branches in the gusty wind.
Nearer the house the silver birch wafted its
Yellow leafed twigs and, with each blustery breeze,
Discarded even more leaves which fell to the ground
Becoming sodden in the water-logged green grass.
Finally the acer showering lashings of crimson leaves
Into the adjacent pool where, supported by the netting,
They formed a brilliant, colourful surface carpet.
Blue, coal and great tits, green-finches and sparrows
Came cavorting for the generous supply of nuts,
Flying hither and thither to satisfy their hunger.
One could spend hours and hours sitting at ease
Whilst patiently watching the natural world run its course.
Such a contented and peaceful conservatory
In which to contemplate - a restful and peaceful sanctuary.

Ada M Witheridge

EVENING ON THE AVON - DESPITE THE BYPASS

Gliding through velvet darkening
squish of mud-foot underfoot
twilight ripples in soft swathes
round my ears a blanket of soundless air descends
and movement detected but no longer seen.

Through the tree shapes water sheen
riverbank silhouettes melt into monochrome
'Quiet down now' nature whispers
'Hush, go to sleep.'

Then startle of white against the gloom
as two swans
dip and curve their necks
in mute pas de deux; adagio
diving for last morsels of the day
gracefully unaware of the blessing
they bring to my tired heart.

Rachael Clyne

RIVER SKELL

Ancient three arched stone-bridge,
hardly visible now,
over the River Skell.
Elaborate old stone
arches must have once been
important route to and
from somewhere - commerce -
came to rest?

Bridge erratically
used now by farmers - if
at all. Highway away -
now separate - so this
once busy thoroughfare
is now shared by wild-life,
ramblers, journeying
peace seekers.

Robert D Shooter

VESPERELLA

The vespers whispered danger to the soul
Engulfing the cinder track,
Suggesting another route home.
But I could have sat behind a desk all day
And safely watched a part of me
Die anyway.
I thought it strange that a man
Half turning at my noise
Veered off the track,
Them, seeing me and righting himself
Should move directly into my path.
I thought his dog had more manners
And showed more sense, stopping
To peer myopically into my one
Frail light.
Then I realised it was not me,
But another dog he was wary of,
Looming up at him from the
Encroaching night.
Does this path, unlit and overgrown
Compare to your road to heaven?
It is sought out by the few, true,
And has its perils,
But it's so much shorter,
More direct
Than the fume laden, bus dodging
Tarmac trek.

Gail Vernon

NOT IN ENGLAND (TIME TRAVEL)

The immeasurable city sprawled like galaxies into greenbelt
and images of shopping trolleys as houses take over;
vast concrete condominiums and cows sharing fields.

The rickety journey through a space age idea,
the green fields stretching on and on with no sign of sea
and that's it for twenty minutes of darkness.

I talk past you at my reflection in the window
I am inside and outside. Where
are the white cliffs when you need a reminder?

So, we take a journey to the buffet,
just like the '80's cocktail bar that thought it was Futurist
and the ground comes up to greet me.

A twenty minute journey? But we're already
an hour ahead. Time's a peculiar thing.
We advance regardless at 3 miles a minute.

We break through those unseen boundaries,
as the light at the end of the tunnel
bursts open like a slap in the face.

France. And without any signs in sight,
it looks just like England. Without the eighteen ducklings.
In a dream we race the cabbage fields to the end.

Ruth Bettany

WOODLAND

Along by the reservoir
Over the dancing stream
By way of the stepping stones
To the woodland of my dreams.

Tall yellow archangel
With giant golden heads
Silver birch glistening
By the pond,. long green reeds.

Wind rustling through the leaves
Birds heard, but seldom seen
Dappled sunlight - welcome shade
Everywhere I see green.

The scent of the earth
The warm, yielding bark of redwoods
Granite boulders with lichen
It all feels so good.

Lyn Richard

FRENCH RESTAURANT

Entrez, donc . . .
The door opens outwards; warm air gushes
redolent of cooking to the street.
Incurious eyes sweep in-comers; conversations
pause; resume: uncomfortably, the people
in the ante-room lift drinks, chew olives.

Now . . .
Check the booking. Patrons at the bar
prevent the survey of the black-clad book.
The maitre d' is harassed, elsewhere occupied,
throwing a stream of comments kitchen-wards,
ticking the hieroglyphics on the page.

A plush-clad bench awaits; pile scratchy to the touch
of fingers settling skirts, deposing bags,
preparing to take up the gastronomic gage
of plastic-coated menu. Sip the drinks;
choose wines and courses, follow through
and up the stairs into the darkened cave
of the main chamber. Votive candles
light tables, complement dried flowers.

Silver glistens, glasses darkly glint,
cupping within them napkins, sombre, red -
no linen lilies here, for all accessories
are up-to-date. The gold and white
and crusty freshness of the petit pain
lies mutely sacrificial on the plate
awaiting butter. Take the place
and courteously smile at partner,
waiter - let the rite begin.

Elizabeth Parish

RAINING AGAIN/WONDERING WHATEVER

it's raining again.
i watch the rain
outside my window.
i see
cars
that look like skaters
on ice.
i don't think that they go around
circling in loops,
but you never know,
are never sure
what goes on
just around the corner,
or past the hedge.
the hedge is a place of
noises and shadows.
before you see
who makes the noises
and who the shadows are,
before those who are the shadows
and those
who make the noises
see my window
and walk on by,
or look in
wondering who or what is
in here.
wondering whatever.

alis rain

BEHIND

I shivered,
As I walked into the room,
It was un-lived,
I cringed at the dust sprinkled windows.
The air was still,
Nothing was moving,
But I felt
Everything moving behind me.
The door creaked shut,
I jumped around,
My heart pounding,
My ears were listening so carefully.
A tap on the window,
I stopped breathing.
Something was there,
I could feel it looking.
It's eyes were deep in me,
I pleaded myself to turn,
To face the horrible creature
I knew was there.
Fear penetrated through me,
Suddenly I could move,
But I ran, ran out of the door
And down the creaking stairs,
And out the banging door,
And I paused
Begging myself to look up.
I could feel it,
Even out in the cold,
It was there, I felt it.

Rebecca Lawrence (14)

QUAINT STREETS

In Ludlow's quaint streets there is plenty to see,
The Feathers for coffee, de Gray's for fine tea.
A trip to the local, a drink and a snack,
A walk to the castle in shirt sleeves or mac.

A few streets are narrow and tell of their age,
When clocks nearby watched over handcart and stage.
The street with its stalls is both handsome and rare.
Imagine the bustle when horses were there.

Some houses are Georgian, some have timbers outside,
And people regard them with love and with pride.
No planners have spoiled them, no precincts are there,
You can stroll to the river and breathe the clean air.

Few streets in this England have not changed a lot,
Yet some are not bothered and don't care a jot.

Gordon Carter

EASTBOURNE...

Ozone, fragrant breath of sea
Happy sunburnt faces
Leaving behind reality
Worries leave line traces.

Every day enjoy
Look and look around you
As your senses you employ
Enjoying now and de ja vu.

Relaxing, lazing, dreaming
Remembering times gone by
Planning daily, scheming
To enjoy each day you try.

And the sunshine is warming
And it's nice to be waited upon
And the sea view is exciting
And who's here when you've gone.

The seagulls scream a welcome
You've come again this year
And when it's time to say goodbye
You'll brush away a tear.

Red arrows swooping, diving
Seaside business easily thriving
Flowered carpets growing well
Even flowers caught in the spell

Sun is shining every day
Rain at night so they say
The pier is long and full of life
Smiling people who've banished strife.

My once a year to Eastbourne's gone
But next year we've another one . . .

Anne Clark

THE HOUSE

The sun shines warmly on the summer street,
a scrawny dog rushes by
as a crowd gathers watching the executioner prepare:
steel monster ready to destroy,
crashing down against the defenceless walls
spraying a cloud of dust which blows
memories away, an old woman wipes away a tear,
she lived there once, but that was long ago.
This house has seen many dramas,
now the curtain has been drawn on the cast.
She remembers sunny summer days like this;
reading in the garden and drinking from a cold glass.
Now there's a hole like an extracted tooth,
the people disperse after the show
that is except for a sad old woman
who lived there once, but that was long ago.

Guy Fletcher

FOR JACKEY'S PEN

I've seen that face again
The one that sets me back
To the classroom noise,
The school-yard jokes,
The local park.

To know then what I know now
To ignore guidance when offered
To lose the chance
The ticket blown away.
Never to return.

Only sadness remains
In a heart yet still alone.
Of what might have been
No. What should have.

I wonder what she thinks
Looking thoughtful, embarrassed.
Am I so unapproachable?
Did I leave such scars?
That hurts more . . .
Than the deepest knife.

Next time we meet may be the last
If a next time comes along
Somehow fate says 'Yes'
On a good day that is.

Paul Davis

THE LOFT

Dad, what's up there?
What is it like?
Dad, can I have a look?
Is it nice?

Dad, give me a hand,
I'm now on the ladder.
Dad, I'm a little bit nervous but
I'd like to go further.

Dad, I'm half way there,
Are you close behind?
Dad, just a few more steps but
The dust makes me blind.

Dad, I'm just at the rim,
It's darker than pitch.
Dad, where can it be?
Where is the switch?

Dad, I've seen it all now,
I've seen every beam.
Girl, it's always the same,
What's unseen is a dream!

Joe Hughes

SIDE STREET

The street was busy with Saturday shoppers,
I dodged the pushchairs and exasperated mothers.
To escape the rush I slipped down a side street,
All of a sudden I had a memory flash.
For all the modernising of the street
This side street was remarkably unchanged.
The narrowness, graffiti on the walls,
Rusty barbed wire on the lamp-posts.
Even the 'fire exit' door was still unpainted,
I remember now this music store used to be a cinema.
I used to queue around the block
And go to all those late night films,
They finished early morning, 6.30am.
My first love and I ran down this side street
We kissed passionately against this wall.
Time was playing tricks on me,
I submerged from the side street
And was caught in the busy flow of pedestrians,
I felt detached from this time, my mind was in the past.

David Medcalf

TO THE HIGH PLACES

It's winter. On the high land nothing stirs,
Except a solitary, slinking fox,
Or pheasant scuttling deep among the firs,
Lamenting now the autumn equinox.

For all things then were clothed in russet-brown,
And tales of summer's raptures still were told;
Now winter brings the hoary curtain down;
The world, like life, looks bleak and very old.

And far across the steeple-studded plain,
In little rashes of humanity,
Pale visions of dead glories light again
The past like sunlight on a placid sea.

Encompassed in the orbit of my eye,
A thousand hamlets shimmer through the haze,
As raw December marches stiffly by;
And one, especially, sets my soul ablaze.

For there, in youth, lived one I fondly knew,
Beneath the shadow of the sombre world,
When vernal joys were ours, and love was true,
And eyes gleamed rapture-bright, and hearts ran gold.

But years so tender slipped away like sand,
Dissolving like a sigh in life's mad race,
And soon I lost her warm and steadfast hand,
Nor breathed again the freshness of her face.

So, from this high place deep among the firs,
I watch the winter clouds like dreams drift by,
Remembering she was mine, and I was hers -
And shall be till the stars fall from the sky.

S H Smith

RADCLIFFE WEIR

High on the cliffs, weir waters whisper.
Behind bushes and saplings the River Trent hides.

Down sloping steps the path to the waters
Jerks and checks walkers as they begin to go down.

Too long or too short, too high or too low,
Carefully designed stairs keep the user's pace slow.

Cheerleader trees, min-skirted by closeness,
Line the sides of this gladiators run.

Canopied and covered the path swings to the right,
No river view yet, but the whisper's now loud.

Like a little dog called to its master
A tiny brook runs towards the sound.

A leaning tree ducked or else to be climbed round
And the smell is strong in the weir-dampened air.

First there's the beach, then there's the wide river
And half way across a fisherman's casting his line.

Blue skies and green fields background the picture
As more and more detail appears in the scene.

Here's the weir now, bounded this side by concrete,
And held prisoner the other, by the brick wall of a lock.

Moored motor-boats bob as barges approach.
They enter the lock and wait to pass through.

On the far bank couples stroll along slowly,
And a man in a deck chair sleeps by his car.

Defiant, death-daring, barefoot boys balance,
Tight-roping the weir's lip and walking its weeds.

And just beneath them the foam and froth splashes
And rainbows arch up and into the air.

The shouts that the boys make are quickly silenced
As the weir's white noise creates its own peace.

R L Cooper

SUNSETS

The sun that sets on the open sea,
Gives its reflection, a calmness to see.
A golden glow in the evening sky;
The end of the day that has gone by.

The sun that sets behind a mountain,
Sends its rays down like a falling fountain.
Majestic shadows creeping across the land;
The darkness of dusk as if painted by hand.

The sun that sets so early in the desert,
Leaving a blackening cold until it reverts,
Once again to climb high above the sand,
With a warm breeze that moves like a fan.

The sun that sets deep in the forest,
Casting its long fingered shadow to digest,
The warmth of the day and the golden embers,
Leaving its branches drenched with evening tremors.

The sun that sets all over the world,
Leaving us all wreathed in a glow unfurled.
The miracle of the day and night abound,
Gradually sinking slowly without a sound.

Valerie Marshall

MY ENGLAND ISLE

I love my country, gave me my home.
Lovely changing seasons where truth is shown.
She is my England, my joy and my pride,
See the wonder of her changing seasons,
You'll find all the answers, all the reasons.

Spring will be here soon,
Goodbye, winter's tune.
Today, all in harmony,
On this my island home.

I love my island, she has a heart.
Reminding me of mama, never far apart.
Teaching all the lessons only nature can show.
From birth to death she tells us ever knowing.
Tells us of a life that's ever growing.
Everything's alive, nothing ever dies.
A soul of love goes on and on
Like mama's smile.

God bless you and keep you, my England Isle.

M Millard Bradley

PRESTON DOCKS

Old photos show them at the opening of the Docks,
Those Late Victorian workmen. They lean
On pickaxe handles in the sun,
Bearded, Sunday waistcoats on, their wives in frocks.
Out-shouldering Aldermen for our attention.

The river's silted artery killed the Docks.
Land-locked, anachronistic as the red ran from the map,
The port became a sink for Swedish timber, Spanish fruit
And, for us, a remembered elsewhere, where an uncle worked
Or where, on New Year's Eve, the ships' horns sounded,
                    less lament now, more benediction.

Jim Patten

SHALL THIS BE THE LAST TIME THAT I SEE IRELAND

Loud searching sounds the bird struggles to rise, lighter
easier now she rises into the sky.
A fullness fills my ears and a delight within my heart
at the wonder down below. A reservoir of size, the
glistening of the motor cars, like specks upon the road as
I between the layer of cloud on looking down the little
fields of many shapes and sizes.
Floating clouds in a near perfect sky as we rise higher
still, it is strange the feeling on each trip home.
'Will this be the last time that I see Ireland.'
Above the clouds I rise in flight, milky great dense
things, no patched worked fields but clustered towns and
rambling river seen through the odd gap where flying
clouds separate.
Another town I see, for blue is sky like mid summer and
we are yet in spring, high and higher still we rise.
Sun reflected on the cloud as if on snow, shading greys
to a lovely pink on the moving crystal coloured cloud,
I follow this arrangement until it gets smaller as I stare harder
on the point of fainting I have to stop.
Tea arrives. Blindness of the brightness of the fluffy
clouds without any break, again I ride the large white
cloud and it has always held me intrigued with its
ever changing picture in a faster moving time.

A sentimental traveller with a lovely mind.

Margaret Gleeson Spanos

A Quiet Storm

A silent wind was blowing calmly through the trees
Gradually building up strength, changing into a breeze.
A strange sound of whistling as it was slowly getting strong
In the silence of the night was the birth of a quiet storm.
Clouds sailing across the sky then suddenly breaking apart
Followed by rain tumbling down strong as a beating heart.
A sudden clap of thunder echoing across the skies
A flash of lightening so blinding before my very eyes.
In the distance of the night a quiet storm was born.

The night stood still and all was once again calm.
Only the softness of a silent wind brushing against my face.
Suddenly a crackle of thunder ripped me with fear,
So frightening, as I ran, a quiet storm once again was here.
With stillness in the air, with darkness in the skies,
A quiet storm was fading silently before my eyes.
An eerie night was slowly coming to an end,
The storm seemed over, the awakening of the dawn.
A final end to a quiet storm.

The tempest has finally ended
The moon stood still
Silence was in the air
The night again at peace
A quiet storm eventually ceased.

Graham Macnab

SKETCHES OF SKIPTON

Sculpted in stone, worn by water
the town is walled in dought
and diligence, framed by the ribbed
and rolling hills of mightier creation.

> The feet of men have trod this path
> before our fathers flagged the earth,
> and ancient ways still intersect
> amongst the market stalls.

In secret courts an archway beckons
trailing trace of sweet aromas;
echoes flit like memory
down a flight of granite steps.

> The calm canal and patient trees
> await the still of evening as
> a thrush calls from the castle yard
> as we set pen to paper.

John Carley

A HOLIDAY PARADISE

Rows of umbrellas whose colours bright,
Stretch in horizontal line,
Along the golden sand,
While lovers stroll the sea shore,
In their own world slowly,
Hand in hand.

From the sea waves lap onto the beach,
White froth at the feet,
Soon to disperse,
Bikini clad the women sunbathe,
Hot bodies in sun cream,
They immerse.

Children play by throwing stones,
Searching and finding shells,
Which they collect,
While the elderly sleep in deep contentment,
Dreaming of their lives,
In retrospect.

Overhead the seagull on the wing,
Upon the therm,
Glides high,
With palms that reach their fronds,
That for years have sought,
The sky.

Boats rock gently to and fro,
As pleasure cruisers,
Call in port,
This paradise their own,
Each holiday maker,
Has sought.

Ann G Wallace

THE GARDEN SWING

The roses crown the pergola in swathes of pink perfection,
Their heady scent perfumes the air in every direction.
I brush the lavender as I pass,
Admire its purple flowers,
I sniff the scent of new mown grass,
And think about the hours
Of sowing seed, of rain and sun, of work and patient waiting
To bring about this miracle that nature is creating.

Despite the work, despite the toil,
The labouring in the heavy soil,
The cutting, pruning, wielding shears,
My aching back and ageing years,
When I get home from work at night
There in the garden is my delight.
The garden swing which beckons me
Is where, all day, I've yearned to be.

I sit a while and sip my tea admiring the border
Guilty with the knowledge that the rest is not in order.
Yonder is a wilderness of nettles, weeds and brambles,
Haven for the wildlife that in it lives and rambles.
Butterflies and hedgehogs, a cheeky little bird,
To change all this for groomed delight would really be absurd.
I lay back on the cushions and hear the birds that sing,
I already see perfection from my seat upon the swing.

M D Reader

HOLLYWELL'S ARBORETUM

Tucked away in a corner of Hollywell's park is a walled paradise.
Gravel paths criss-cross the flower beds
and little wooden benches, sit secluded between small evergreens.
From a child, I've sat there
in a pocket of peace . . .

Time doesn't go there.
Worries halt at the gate.
and the air is always rich with perfumes.
In winter, the old north winds prowl the walls
but has to be content to howl at the gates . . .

But you should go there in the summer
it's one square of Heaven, fell to the Earth.
From June to August, she's a Victorian Paradise.
Pale roses and green grass.
With white clad ladies and gentlemen
playing bowls in the long evenings . . .

If you were lucky enough to sit alone here
you may sense the small hand of a child
wrapped gently by your own
or hear its distant laughter a little clearer.
Here, where the world leaves room for such things.
Go there. Sit there, and wait
for the magic to come upon you.

N D Potter

THE PLACE WE'D MEET

I want to sit with you again and talk
Under the old oak
When summer's in full blaze;
Where the wind whispers
With first finger to lips
And small finger to ear of ground;
Where the sun plays games with the light -
With a golden veil
That shimmers the distant city
So it appears as smoke.

The tree still remains -
Timeless in a world of chaos
But only summons I,
Though, when beneath,
The branches span the years that distance you -
They summon memories of better times -
Times that only fade with sun
- When the mind's like tired pages -
Or near dizzy heights where spirits climb.

John Hill

A Sense Of Cheshire

Can you smell the sound of autumn showing?
Listening to the ripened tastes bursting.
As the days darken in early shadows,
Wood-smoke meanders through misty dew.

Silently, the muffled sunset lowers,
Darkens reds, fallen gold.
Stewed leaves slide down rain-drenched lanes,
Whilst deadwood crackles gloriously underfoot.

Saluting horns from Canada Geese,
Form fallowed lines astride stubbbled lea,
Ensnare the senses in harvest burning -
Before too late - the season dies.

Pat Derbyshire

AT SEVEN

As seven, I saw London torn apart
Through the experience and eyes of a child.
I saw the urban landscape changing
Every day as I watched
From the over-ground tube
Travelling to Willesden via Harlesden and Stonebridge Park.

The landscape changed as I was watching.
One image it evoked in me
Was of a mouth, losing, painfully shedding
Those that belonged.
Each day the jaw and the city were experiencing
The dentist's art of extraction.

Kate Sumner

FROM LOWER TO HIGHER

I stepped in; following others.
The darkness inside took me by surprise -
My eyes had to adjust
To the lack of light in the Sacré-Coeur.
It took a while until I could see.

See people, quietly moving about.
See strangers, lighting white candles.
Meditating. Praying.
I sat down taking it all in.
'Please be silent' I read on the wall.

Do respect the meaning of it all.
I was in another world.
I got up; went to the souvenir shop.
Hidden behind stone pillars;
I bought a necklace - a tiny wooden cross

Tied to a thin strip of leather.
The symbol of it all.
I bought a ticket to go up to the Dome.
Climbed the spiral staircase with difficulty.
Those old steps

Half killed me. Narrow and steep,
They went round and round.
Up and up. Never ending. Never ending.
At last I reached the top; the light.
From such heights, what a view!

Paris was there, before me.
Under a clear blue sky.
Looking amazingly beautiful,
In the early morning sun. Paris . . .
City of love.

Claire-Lyse Sylvester

CHANGE

My footsteps led me back one day
To the house where I was born,
To look at that old-world garden
Enclosed in a high brick wall.
Where I played magic games of childhood
'Midst the flowers that stood so tall.

I could scarcely wait to find the gate
And recapture my youth again,
A lifetime sped, on wings had fled,
But my journey was all in vain.
For such is fate, I'd left it too late,
Now all I had left was pain.

Oh, Joyous childhood! Can it be,
That all that is left for memory. Is
A cleared space - without a trace,
Of the happiness you brought to me!

Ivy Cawood

DELHI INDIA

I saw silver street . . . A three ringed circus.
A native bazaar stretched to the mile.
A sense of excitement, a certain enlightenment
And I suddenly felt the need to smile.

I tasted from booths . . . Displaying sweetmeats,
Titillating taste buds to the extreme.
With sugared coats in copper pans,
Forgetting my waistline as if in a dream.

Grain stores with its wheat and barley
Corn and millet piled on high
Cardamom sesame, various spices
The aroma of ghee on the fry.

Sugar cane shearers, going clickety click
The chatty barbers, clip, clip, clip.
The tailors' scissors with their snip, snip, snip
Sitting in his Buddha's pose.
The thud, thud, thud of silver and gold
Pressed and beaten for threaded clothes.

Crowded streets, the smell of leather
A jostling laughing wedding group,
Bobbing weaving two wheeled ekkas,
Good natured confusion . . . A carnival troupe.

A beggar child with pleading eyes,
Clothes tattered and torn in shredded array.
The rich man with his airs and graces,
I felt I had seen the world in a day.

Doreen Welby

DREAMING IN ACHARSEID MOR
('The big harbour' on a small island)

Sitting
    In afternoon sun
    Warm wood under bare toes toasting.

Silence
    Increased by a distant discussion of gulls.

Breeze
    Blows softly over arms no longer clad
    defensively in damp synthetic fur.

Reading
    Adrian Henri
    In the streets of Liverpool
    Seeing the Spring in plastic daffodils.

Seaweed
    Hangs brown and yellow over children's caves.
    Thick heavy hair for half tide rocks
    That come and go like mermaids.

Seal
    Teapot tilted on its seaweed rock.
    Soaking in sun.
    Shortsightedly sniffing round the air-filled world.

Silence
    The clearances come clear through Calum's Fiddle.
    Every event, with the dignity of design,
    Deserving the duty of the dance.

Bill Waugh

THE GRAND CANYON

The dawn was slowly breaking
The sun rising above the rim.
Revealing the majestic Grand Canyon
As the mists began to thin.
I held my breath in wonder.
On sacred ground I trod,
As sun-rays pierced the darkness
I saw the handiwork of God.

A myriad of colours
Danced on the surface of the stone.
And lifted my spirit skywards
Into creation, and beyond.
The shimmering glow of colours
Changing, ever, constantly,
Played upon the ancient rocks
Like a glorious symphony.

My whole being was suffused with awe
To embrace this glory, unfurled.
I heard the music of Angels
In this new and Heavenly world.
This miracle of beauty
Made eternity seem near,
I felt a wondrous, golden presence
That moved my heart to tears.

I stood transfixed in rapture
The river sparkling, far below
And knew, that this mystical place of splendour
Would, forever, haunt my soul.

Jessica Jordan

SONG FOR A SEAGULL

A seagull circles my house
solitary and white
it makes no cry

It scribes for me another sky - extravagantly blue
above a bay of splintered light where I with hunter's eye
cast the spinning lure into a green black mackerel sea

Or watched the oyster catchers wade and stitch
scalloping the edges of the pools
under the luggers lying angled in the sand

Beneath a granite tower gull-girdled to the flagpole
whose tongue belled from its bed
each psalm-hung Sabbath in a pagan spring

White cottages in cockled creeks where herons roost
and curlew cries and tall trees whisper tales at dusk
to children running in the tamarisk

(An idyll for two lovers - an agony for one)

Long rollers with two thousand miles of reach
forever break their backs on the stacked granite
gaining but a grain or two to build a beach
a handful in a century

Where once I brought my poem of hunger, hope and pain -
and love - that bubble which must every day be blown anew
to break upon the rock of her indifference.

(For crumbs are not beach enough for comfort
and centuries are for seashells)

A seagull circles my house
solitary and white
this cry I make.

Lee Sheldrake

THE VILLAGE CHURCH

The ancient grave stones loom stark and grey
Whilst the salt sea wind bites my bones.
The brave crocuses carpet the mossy ground
with a haze of blue, and seagulls call to the
souls of the dead.

The tiny church crouches by the edge of
the stormy sea
Timeless and squat.
High above on a gaunt cliff an
earlier, ruined chapel broods in sombre silence,
A monument to a distant past.

The coffin is lowered into the frozen earth.
A church bell tolls.

I stand lost in reverie at the mercy of
the icy, relentless wind
Remembering my wedding at this simple church.
The summer sun was shining then and warm
sunbeams danced on the sparkling, indigo sea.

I draw my thick, black cloak close to my
shivering body and retrace my steps for home.

Joan Mackereth

AT BUDDS WALL BEDHAMPTON

I heard the mud singing as I stood on the shore
Seagulls crying their wild free call.
Seaweed green, cockles spitting,
Boats resting on the mud.
Sea winds blowing, grasses on the bank
Whispering to themselves.
And far away the distant roar of traffic on the roads.
A kestrel hovered overhead.
A skylark sang high in the blue sky.
So wild and free this place
And it has not changed since I was a little girl.

Jennifer M Trodd

IN MY GLORY

When I looked upon Bertha
its people came not to admire
but to pillage and to plunder,
to hunt the deer and cut my
foliage down.

Once my feet bathed in the Tay,
where the ice gathered in winter
and in the summer sun
its cool clear water ran.
Then the people came.

As Bertha grew and changed its name.
And still the people came,
not in my glory to share
but to strip me bare.
Thus dawned my darkest day.

Laid waste my splendour the deer
long gone, my foliage now only
heather, yet still the people came,
to graze their sheep and wonder
for no more had I to plunder.

Time heals my sores, the deer
and trees return and in the summer sun
once again my colours glow,
for mow the people come not to reap
but to sow.

Now as I look down upon
this fair city of Perth,
and still the people come
not to pillage or to plunder
but to share with me my splendour.

Robert Wilkie

TORRE ABBEY SANDS

Soft on the shell-struck morning sand
The sun's rays toss their diamonds down
To rest in furrows near the surf
Where sand-worms cast their spiralled mounds.

Within the rock pools, deep and warm
The pale crabs glide from stone to stone
Beneath a floating tress of weed
Where small subaqueous creatures roam.

From high above the plaintive gulls
Swoop to inspect the virgin beach,
Cleansed by the night-long ebb and flow
With sea-strewn debris rearranged.

Driftwood and pebbles, weed and shells,
The tide creates a vast collage
Sequinned with sand and spiced with brine
Cast on the canvas of the shore

While ceaselessly, like time itself
The soporific sound is heard
Of waves that spill in slow caress
To leave a glistening strip of land.

Janette Coombe

Dawn

Silver grey; the frosty dawn
Creeps stealthily over the fells;
The trees silhouetted against the awakening sky
Reach out to touch the morning.
A mist so fine, draws a curtain of gossamer
Across the face of Blencathra.
The rosy blush of the rising sun
Heralds the dawn's glory.

A R Bailey

SURVIVAL OF THE SKYLARK

I stand here at the bus stop, briefly in rapture
Remembering as a child, this concrete as pasture
Over broken gate, through golden grass swaying
A message by song, the skylark conveying

Poppies like children in red hats dancing
Seemed to stop and pause - intermittently glancing
Insects took flight - tactually we'd amble
Avoided spiders webs, whilst plucking the bramble

Grasshoppers leapt as we tried to ensnare
Approached tethered horse - seeing who'd dare
My dreams then broken by late bus arrival
One note from the skylark as if announcing survival.

Keith Dickinson

BRITAIN'S GLORY

How quiet down Devon's lane:
no man-made sound
but a far off plane.

The trees overhang, casting dappled shade
in childhood past
under these we played.

These hedgerows abound with wildflowers fair:
campion, buttercup and violets so sweet
are there.

Birds are feeding their young in the hedge
rushing to and fro
waiting for them to fledge.

As harder they work, the birds never complain
as they graft all day
in this quiet country lane.

Honeysuckle, the sweetest of briars:
the scent of which
your nostril never tires,

entangles its shoots of vibrant green
its pink and yellow flowers
a beauty as seen.

Of all the many glories of Britain
to me Devon's best
of that I'm certain.

Bessie

THIS BLESSED LAND, THIS ENGLAND

I love this country of my birth, this land of great renown,
This monarch realm, like vintage wine, her old and ancient towns.
I love her veins of rivers, running wild across her breast,
Tumbling through her rolling hills, to find its seaward quest.
I love her quiet country life, her tranquil solitude,
The to and fro in bustling towns, the crazy multitude.
I love her highways, lined with trees, holding hands above my head,
The crunch of fallen autumn leaves, that mighty trees have shed.
I lover her dawn when I awake, I love her moon at night,
The chorus of the singing birds, that greet me with delight.
Yet when I think, with furrowed brow, of answers to her past,
Who was it waved that magic wand, in which my land was cast?
Who carved her from the continent, to bathe in seas alone?
Who fashioned her with loving hands, who set her sceptred throne?
And with perfection in their mind, who built this pleasant land?
With earth so green and floral scene, who was the master hand?
A jewel set in silver seas, old fashioned she may be,
But England, my dear England, means all the world to me.

Thomas Victor Healey

Rhossilli

Peaceful and warm
So full of freshness
The sea calm today
Worm's Head you may walk
When the tide is out
But once in, you may be stranded
To explore and walk Worm's Head
So exhilarating and peaceful
A pure pleasure Worm's Head
The beach view of Worm's Head, *'brill!'*
Rhossilli for sure perfection
Camping up above the beach
Visit the beach by day
Visit the beach by night
Any time that takes your fancy.
Hear the sound of the sea
Smell the freshness of the air
Cool nights, just enjoy Rhossilli
Mewslade Bay a little stroll from
the main beach.
Rocks and caves to explore, just brill.
The village of Rhossilli
Peaceful, pleasant, beautiful
and so warming.
Visit this heavenly place
Rhossilli, South Wales.

David J Hall

FLATTENDEN WADHURST

Our house by the stream was ancient and bold
But brought happy days, as my tenth year rolled.
I loved each moment of walks in the wood.
Paddles in water, whenever I could.

Three miles to school we walked each day
Sometimes coming home, the train crossed our way.
Down there by the stream, the kingfisher flew
His nest full of bones in the bank we all knew.
The dragonflies come, the little voles too
Anemones grow, in the trees, doves coo.
Bluebells grow mid the trees, a beautiful sight
A fox sometimes calls, in the dark of the night.

Childhood memories of nature galore,
And beauty all round, just outside the door.
I'll never forget the mem'ries from then
The happiest days, in old Flattenden.

Edith Buckeridge

MEMORIES ARE MINE

I wandered the fields as I did when a lad
In the village where I was born;
There were moments of joy and some quite sad
On this glorious autumn morn.

The memories of all those years ago
Return as if yesterday,
I felt not alone, but that I could go
With my friends where we had often strayed.

The hedges were lower and no longer 'laid'
Gaps - where once there had been trees;
With modern methods there's a price to be paid,
Mechanisation - if you please.

I avoided the ruts and hoof imprints
Where horse and cart had travelled,
Over earth of clay and stone and flint
And patches of gravel.

The droveway links pastures green
By stile and gate alike,
Beware of ditch - not always seen
But could well cause a fright.

Two towering beech trees still stand real proud
And holly bush nearby,
But disease had destroyed the majestic elms
That used to 'hug' the sky.

Wildlife surrounds and watches you
On wing and ground alike,
A stranger in their midst - out of the blue,
You are watched till out of sight.

Walk on and on through scenery fine
'Soak' up the atmosphere,
The years have passed, the sights are mine
For all you hold most dear.

Brian R Russ

At Dunn's River Falls, Jamaica

They come in shoals to climb the falls
In tourist uniform of pumps and smalls
And, crude hint of the debonair,
A red hibiscus in the hair -

Americans: old, young, large, small,
Determined to enjoy themselves and all
Too confident and free to be
Concerned about their dignity.

Not so their sable, local guides
Who lead them with sure-footed strides;
Respecters only of the strong
You catch them bleakly looking on.

They link their charges' willing hands
And tow them upwards from the sands
Through pools, past rock-falls, all the way
Encouraging their infants' play

Who clamber up and slither down,
Direct their cinés, holler, clown.
Each seems to pay a hackneyed part
With debased words known off by heart.

About the top the vendors' shacks
Are stuffed with useless knicks and knacks,
And there of course for everybody
Ices, Cokes and Nutty-buddy.

But still the banyan lends it shade,
The frangipani flowers invade
The air with scent; and soaring high
The palms sail in the distant sky.

On dry boughs lizards in the sun
Unblinking puff their throats, then run
Like droplets. Below hens scratch, and cock
Whose crow implies now no rebuke.

Ian Bramley

THE MAGIC WOOD

I gazed in wonder at the scene
Of silvery blue on trees once green
Frost that had fallen thick as snow
Was glistening and gleaning on every bough.

A bluey haze hovered around the air
Creating magic that was beyond compare
The silvery boughs brought back to me
Shimmering lights round the Christmas tree.

Excited as a child on Christmas morn
I waited, waited to see the unicorn
In a make-believe world utterly lost
Lost in the tranquil beauty of the frost.

I recall in wonder that beautiful scene
Of silvery blue on trees once green
The bluey haze hovering around the air
Creating such magic that was beyond compare.

Joyce Morris

SUCH A PLACE!

Have you ever thought how lucky we are to live in such a place,
where we can walk with fields in view and the wind upon one's face!

To see a pheasant strutting across the stony ground,
to hear a tractor pulling the plough with that old familiar sound.

To see horses graze in fields, some with their riders going by
to hear and see many birds flying thru' the sky.

My favourite stroll sees much of this, with woods not far away,
a beautiful church with views from a hill across green where
                                                  children play.

How many of us realise the pleasure it gives us all
that where we live and work each day, it's here at Coney Hall.

Tricia Rozze

PRAY FOR ME

There's a world out there, Lord
That I'm trying hard to find,
Love, hope and comfort and someone
who is kind.
'Cos, there's a world out there, Lord
with their riches, I can see.
But, who would care a jolt for this,
and give me sympathy.

For I am just a street child
And I don't know where it's at
Just fighting for a living, beside
that luxuriating cat.
And my coat ain't long and fur-lined,
no warmth, against the cold.
For all I've got is tatters, some cast-offs,
rough and old.

For you see, I'm just a poor street kid,
shovelling piles of trash.
And maybe if I'm lucky, I'll earn,
a little cash.
Going thro' that rubbish tip, 'cos there's no school
for the likes of me.
With no rich, or glamorous parents,
I don't get nowt, for free.

For I'm just a street kid, Lord.
Out all weathers, you all see.
Just an 'insignificant' person,
Lowly born, to *poverty*.

Sue Williams

MY BEACH

I walk along a stormy shore
'neath winter's dark oppressive sky,
A salty cargo on the wind,
a biting cold, a glassy eye.
The thunderous waves beside me crash,
that repetitious dark imposing mass
of churning power beachward bound,
dies at my feet with ne'er a sound,
except for hissing sand and shells
abundant on the ground.
This beach is mine, awakened from its summer rest,
alive and angry, at its best.
A lonely dangerous coastline now,
where ships are smashed from stern to bow.
A place where only weeks before
saw tourists swimming by the score.
That shallow unappreciating mob
who use this bay but rob it of its dignity
by littering within its broad vicinity.
For only now, to see it windswept, wild and grey,
is to witness nature's own awesome inimitable way.

Eric McClurry

STORMY SEAS

Turbulent waters of . . .
        Mighty oceans and seas.
    Ebbing to and fro
        On our shores, to eternity.

Out over the vast darkness,
        Of endless waters deep;
    Currents ever-changing,
        With constant swirl and sweep.

At one, with the elements of storm,
        Great waves crash and roar;
    In wild abandon, foaming high
        They hit the shore.

Wind's piercing scream,
        The powerful surge of the sea;
    Over the Earth
        To infinity; Wild and free . . .

No force compares, with that
        Of mighty seas and oceans deep;
    Shrouded in ageless mystery,
        The darkest depths, their secrets keep.

Maureen Annette Norman

ISLAND OF DREAMS

Come, sail with me
To my Island of Dreams,
Where the sun shines in splendour,
Where everglades seem to be
Havens of peace, no noise
and few cars,
With sheep in the pasturage,
Sea birds and cows.

Come, let's gather wool
For to spin and to weave;
We'll kneel in the Abbey
Till candlelight's eve.
With the blue of the sea
And the shining white sand,
We'll linger a while in
This beautiful land.

We'll bounce on the heather,
Dip into the well
And intercede, daily,
For all those who dwell
In the fever of life,
For their sadness, their pains;
Do come to my beautiful
    Island of Dreams.

Winifred Mary Richardson

NORTHERN AUSTRALIA

At the edges cathedrals of green plunge
towards an improbable azure where
primordial hazards cruise behind the shark net,
where fingers of mangrove probe the Daintree,
where kookaburras deride the notions of
time and roads. And when the rainforest falters,
red ochre pulses in a landscape dumb with heat.

Never so alive to life, never so alert to death
than here where both are whispering in
the spiniflex; here where wind, water,
earth and fire summon the nomad heart
from half a world away.

J V Galvin

THE WAVES

The wind blowing against my face,
Reminds me of warmer days,
And a feeling that I cannot replace,
Of romanticised happiness.

I look down and close my eyes,
And can still see our footprints,
The sensation is no surprise,
Of ineffectual desire.

Just one deep breath before I leave,
I taste the salt and remember,
The days we had and I believe,
They're secured here by the sea.

Emma Ormond

A Country Stroll Recalled

The morning dew lay soft and new
amidst the surrounding calm,
all around a humming sound
enlivened summer's charm.

As we strode out, all about
the larks burst into song,
the sun beat down, a buzzard soared,
romance was feeling strong.

Love blossomed in the summer breeze,
sheer beauty and budding growth,
the swaying corn, the restless trees,
I reached out, embraced them both.

The radiance in my lover's smile
caused heartbeats fast, no sense of time,
and I could tell in a short while
that I would be in love's rich prime.

For she did stir within my soul
a feeling so divine and whole,
that all was mine for to control,
and heaven shone down upon me.

C J Norton

OUT OF AFRICA

The crocodile sleeps among the riverine flora,
Giant hippopotamus bask in the sun,
Cruise boats travel the Zambezi river,
Another safari day has begun.

The mighty elephants plunder the trees,
Amble along stripping bark, eating leaves.
Trumpeting while destroying the Bush.
Termite hills view this with ease.

African fish eagles, short tail, broad-winged,
Perch together and pair for life,
Kingfishers and hammerheads make lots of noise,
Sensing the barren trees' plight.

The world of nature has won again,
Life and death live side by side,
Baboons jump from tree to tree,
Giraffes stretch their necks to the sky.

Victoria Falls the smoke that thunders,
Its sights make you stand in awe,
White water rafters taking brave risks
To ride rapids more and more.

Elizabeth Hunter

FEATHER FLOWERS

The tree was shabby and winter-grim
and looked among the evergreen
old and depressed, not unlike him
by whom its wretched state was seen.
I noted in dejection how
shivering twig and barren bough
made tortured patterns on a sky
dreary and threatening sleet. So I
turned my back and moved away
a pace or two, but was constrained
to hesitate and turn - and stay.
For now that sad tree entertained
vivacious guests. Already there,
three blue tits and a robin were
preening themselves as four chaffinches
arrived and settled only inches
above my head; and there, aloof,
a blackbird in his formal coat
eyed his host's half-timbered roof,
flexed one wing and cleared his throat.
(Perhaps he had been asked to sing,
though early yet for carolling).
The tree was winter-grim no more
but full of hope and joy, wherefore,
encouraged, I went on my way
under a sky not quite so grey,
because that melancholy tree
had put on *feathered flowers* for me.

Richard Holt

TO REST BESIDE

To rest beside the river's tide
where leaves of autumn take a ride.
To vanish now within the spray,
then travel on some watery way,
until upon some shore abide.

When as the waters rise they glide
back on the river deep and wide,
to seek a sheltered bank or stray
to rest beside.

Withered in the sun well dried
their gaudy autumn colour died.
As winter hues all turn to grey,
upon some frozen earth they lay.
When dead with leaves, I shall reside,
to rest beside.

Ron Grantham

BRIGHTON BEACH MEMORIES

The barefoot terror of the sucking sea
the stones that shift, underneath my shivering
childhood toes, those unseen fish that bite
or nip and cling with dangerous claws;
the rusty tins and men-o'-war from picture books
that hide their stinging tentacles,
and bubbled weed that wraps my ankles
tangling me with tarry slime.
Waves that break the sea groyne, sting
my thin-skinned arm with salt whip,
hasty tides that rush in, unpredictable,
marooning storybook adventurers and shivering
childhood me, dividing me from rescuers
and flasks of tea and swaddling towels and land.

Susan Utting

POPPIES

How the field of poppies bloom
dancing faces red and bright,
So gentle like a tissue paper flower,
like my mother used to make
and place around the room.

As the sun goes down
and the evening breezes blow,
The field of poppies toss their heads
It's time to close the petals,
and rest until the dawn,

When like a bright fire burning
burst into flower for, the new morn
so soft in the morning dew,
as I think of this quiet place
where I feel so close to you.

The redness of each petal,
Blending pink and deeper hue,
Shining as if polished like a
brightly new shoe.

They say for each one of you
there's a body there,
but I just can't believe it
with such scent upon the air.

The only sadness that I feel
when the autumn comes, along,
and the poppy fields lie empty
like a long-forgotten song.

Soon the springtime will return
and I can walk the fields once more,
As we walked together long ago
In the field were poppies grow.

Winifred Thorpe

COLOURS OF THE MIND

Amongst the colours of our mind
Seldom do we find
What we are looking for

Within the depths of the soul
There lies the ultimated goal
That we're all striving for

The mind holds many complex colours
Made up from shades of many others
The art lies in ability
To separate them all and see
Just which colour holds the key
To a door to set us free.

Let all the colours blend together
And we'll sit and wonder whether
We should go this way or that
It seems there's too much to combat

Take the time to realise
One day each colour will arise
To take its turn in our creation
And fill us with deserved elation

All you have to do right now
Is focus hard and allow
The mind to open up to you
To let the colour take its cue

Take a paintbrush in your hand
And sweep this hue across the land
Indulge yourself in its richness
Relieve yourself from the sickness
That has blurred your vision
Causing all this indecision.

Once you are immersed
It cannot be reversed
Your soul will be emancipated
No longer will you feel ill-fated.

Zita Holbourne

FROM SNOWDON'S SUMMIT

I viewed majestic Snowdon, tall
Before me, like a massive wall.
I reached the summit, and I sat
Upon a rock, and marvelled at
The spectacle that I could see:
The lovely island, Anglesey,
Before me, like a map, was spread
From Menai Bridge to Holyhead,
So flat, so different from the land
Around me. On the one hand:
Lakes and hills, and mountains,
Down which springs rushed, making fountains
As they splashed from ledge to ledge
On their way to some lake's edge.
I saw, on the other hand,
Marshy, barren, bleak moorland;
Here and there a steeper slope,
Up which some men climbed using rope.
On looking back to Anglesey,
My father's birthplace I could see -
Beaumaris, jewel of the isle
The fairest town in many a mile.
I looked across the isle to where
Some smoke was rising in the air;
A ship upon the waves was tossing,
From Holyhead to Ireland crossing,
Then mist came down and blocked my sight -
A white sheet had shut out the light.
I called the wind, and I did say:
'Come, Wind, and blow this mist away,
So that once more I may see
That lovely island, Anglesey.'

Roger Williams

YOUR SKY THIS EVENING

The glow, the radiance the colours of your sky Lord
Glowed with such beauty, it would be hard to repeat
Not for you I know, but thank you just the same
For the joy of sight and the ability to witness is sheer delight
Even your geese flew across to enhance the scene
As if to write your signature on this picture
The silhouette of the trees against the sky gave added
Dimension of your ever-living presence
Thank you Lord for the priceless masterpiece before my eyes
To put it onto canvas, I could not capture, but I will try.
I will gladly go into rapture and awe of you
The Master Painter and Maker of our earth, sea and sky.

Joan Marian Jones

THE MEADOWLAND

Just to be able to linger, for such a while, by a rickety well-worn fence,
While stretching forth my eyes, to see beyond all vision, further hence,
Fields enriched in glorious array, with wild flowers, abundantly spread,
Touched now by my fleeting foot over them, which now I duly tread.

The dusty road left so long ago, winding to and fro, straddling to
the field,
But all thought, would the fence hold, my weight upon, which
I duly yield,
My legs were over, encroached the hallowed field, upon the wealth
of flowers,
The sun poured into my heart, of the expected bliss, of
rapture-filled hours.

I could not help but stand on them, how oft I tried not to, as in
abundance lay,
The field in magnificence, was dressed a fine coat, many bright
colours display,
Fragrance was about the place, fell upon my nostrils, wafted on the
pleasant air,
Could the richness of the world, presume as much, to the
meadowland compare.

The prevailing spirit of nature, was in her bower, alive and so
wonderfully well,
The fruits of her passion, in every leaf, and petal, caught up in a
magic spell,
The stillness and the solitude, follows the glorious path, my eager feet
do walk,
Beneath a canopy rich in leafy glade, then I find, a single, ever so
solitary stalk.

Then another comes, rich in colour blue, full upon my appreciative
adoring eye,
Then to my delight, all is revealed, bluebells as far as vision allows,
duly I spy,
Nigh as my feet met the forest floor beyond the meadowland, blanket of
blue,

Shines forth the bluebell, a fairy world, in an enchanted dell, where truth is held true.

Stalks of pure absolute delight, sends in a moment of time, as they all but reel,
I would lay me down about, to breath that magic air, as all around them feel,
To dwell but for a while captivated as I am, caught up in this wondrous domain,
In the grip of some spell, by a Fairy rapture, my Earthly spirit, held so to remain.

But return I must, over the rickety fence, the open road, with backward glance,
Lost the wood, o'er stretches of field, with flowers still, as if held in a trance,
The conjuring of the captured air, touched softly by the stillness of the breeze,
Held the message in the air, of the *bluebells,* secretly nestled, within the trees.

Ross Alexander Omand

THE YELLOW FLAG (IRIS)

Tall, proud, defiantly yellow,
Resonating the rays of noonday sun,
She stands in deep embrace of river bank.
Long spears of deepest green,
Surround her, protect her,
Fending grasping hands of boisterous stream.
Elephantine lobes caress the balmy air,
Whilst golden tongues promise
Rewards to those who dare to enter.
Nodding to the gentle breeze,
She beckons passing bumble bees
Who brave the causeway to her honeyed store
And bent back, re-emerge
Gartered with pollen jewels.
She knows the kingfisher and dragonfly
The stickleback, the vole, the water rat
She signals the wind,
Waves warning to them all
Until, with passing summer, she strikes colour
And tall and proud no more,
Submits and yield's to winter's cold demand.

Mike Cohen

INFORMATION

We hope you have enjoyed reading this book - and that you will continue to enjoy it in the coming years.

If you like reading and writing poetry drop us a line, or give us a call, and we'll send you a free information pack.

Write to :-
    Poetry Now Information
    1-2 Wainman Road
    Woodston
    Peterborough
    PE2 7BU
    (01733) 230746